Contents

How do you get about?

There are many different ways of getting about. You can:

- Walk
- Go by bike
- Go by car
- Go by bus or **tram**
- Go by train
- Go by boat
- Go by plane.

If you are walking, there are **public** footpaths to follow and signposts to show the way.

- Why does the footpath above have metal bars at the end?
- What things help people to find the way?
- What is good about walking, and what is not so good?

Other forms of **transport** help us to go faster and further and to carry heavy things.

- What colours are buses where you live?
- What do you think 'Fast Cat' stands for in the picture below?

Boats and planes take people across the sea.

7

Walking in town

When you walk in town, you are called a **pedestrian**. In towns, most roads have pavements to keep pedestrians separate from **vehicles**.

WHERE YOU LIVE
Look for all the things that help pedestrians in your main street.

- What are the pavements like in your town or village centre?
- Where do you see a pavement surface like the one below?
- How does it help people who do not see well?

The pavement above is made from paving stones. Black posts mark the edge of the pavement.

In the street above, the pavement is higher than the road. The edge of the pavement is called the **kerb**.

•What happens to the kerb at the pelican crossing above?

•Why is the kerb made like that?

•Which types of crossing are in your town?

Pedestrian crossings are safe places to walk across a road. Two types of crossing are a **pelican crossing** (top) and a footbridge (right).

Bridleways and cycle paths

A **bridleway** is a path for horse riders, but walkers may use it too. The white post below is a bridleway marker.

Bridleway:
walkers,
horse riders
& cyclists only

- Why is the bridleway muddy?
- Which other people can use this bridleway?
- On the bridleway marker below, what is the symbol at the top?

In the countryside and in towns, there are paths for cyclists. The symbols on a round blue road sign show who is allowed to use the path.

Some busy roads have a separate **lane** that only cyclists may use.

- Why do some people like to cycle?
- Why is it good to keep cyclists separate from other vehicles?
- What do the markings on the cycle lane mean?

WHERE YOU LIVE
Look for places where cyclists can park their bicycles.

Roads

Roads are links between places.

Some roads are a little wider than a car. Some have room for vehicles to travel in both directions. **Motorways** have several lanes for vehicles going in each direction.

On a road map, different colours are used for different types of roads.

- What types of places are shown by a road sign with a brown background?
- What do motorists have to be careful about when driving along a country lane?
- Why is it usually quicker to use a motorway than a country lane?

WHERE YOU LIVE
Use a road map and
its key to find which
types of roads link
your town or village
to other places.

Vehicles on the road

The first motor cars were made less than 120 years ago. They could not go fast, and few people had a car.

It is very different now. Huge numbers of people travel by road, in cars, taxis, vans, lorries, buses, coaches and on motorbikes.

As the number of motor vehicles grows, roads are widened and new roads are built.

- What is the furthest place you have travelled to by road?
- Do you think roads spoil the countryside?
- Where could the vehicle on the left be going?

Motor vehicles are helpful, but they can also cause problems.

All motor vehicles have an engine to make them go. The engine works by burning a fuel, such as petrol. Unfortunately, this makes fumes, which **pollute** the air.

•Why do lorries come into the town centre?

•What problems can they cause?

WHERE YOU LIVE
Ask the members of your family how much they spend on fuel every week.

Traffic in the town

Traffic drives through the centre of many towns or villages, on its way to other places. It is called 'through traffic'.

But some towns or villages have a **bypass** nearby. Through traffic uses the bypass. People only drive in to the town or village if they want to stop there.

In some main streets, no traffic at all is allowed.

- What type of vehicle is on the through traffic sign?
- Where does traffic go if it is not allowed in the main street?

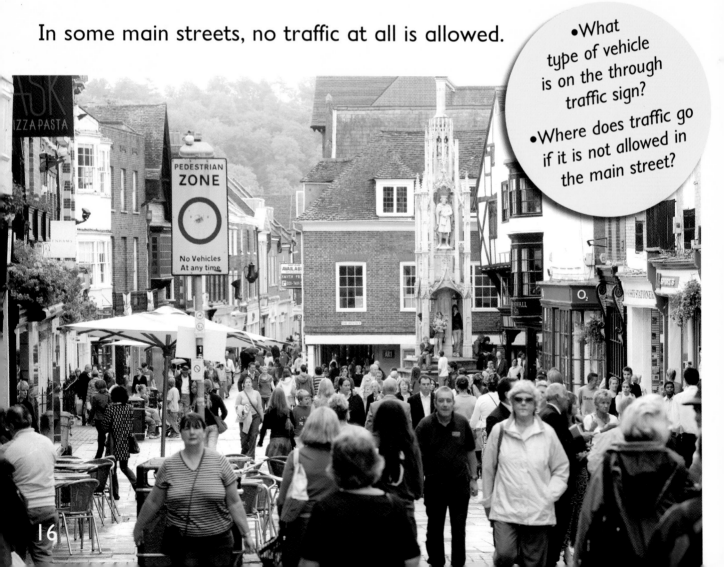

This sign tells people
not to drive faster
than 20 miles per hour.

•Why
should traffic drive
slowly through a village
or town centre?
•Have you used a park and
ride scheme?
•What do people pay for
in the park and ride
scheme below?

WHERE YOU LIVE
Find out what people
think about traffic in your
town or village centre.

A park and ride scheme helps
people to get to a town centre
without their cars.

People park in a
large car park
on the edge of
town. A bus
takes them to
the town centre.

Buses and trams

Buses, trams and trains are types of **public transport**.

- Where do buses go to from your town or village?
- What are bus shelters like where you live?
- What is good and what is bad about going by bus?

People can use a **timetable** (left) to find out when and where a bus stops. They can get on or off the bus at any stop.

They buy a ticket for the journey they want to make. Older people have a **bus pass**.

WHERE YOU LIVE
Use timetables to plan a journey by public transport to your favourite place.

•What do you think it would be like on the top deck of this old tram?

• Have you ever travelled by tram? If so, where?

The first buses and trams were pulled by horses. Modern buses and trams have engines. Bus engines use **diesel** fuel. Tram engines use electricity, from wires overhead.

In busy towns and cities, buses often run on bus lanes. Trams run on tracks in the street.

Going by train

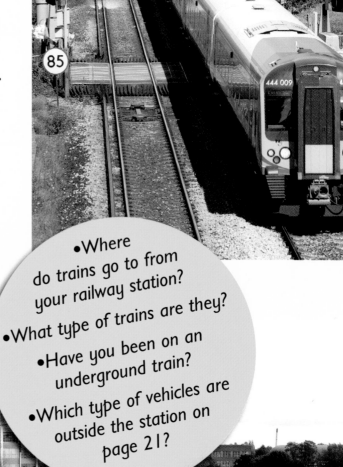

You go to a railway station if you want to travel by train.

Some trains are powered by electricity. Some have a diesel engine. Some carry **passengers**. Others carry **goods**.

On maps and signposts, the symbol for a railway station is a picture of two railway tracks, with two arrows.

Charing Cross

- Where do trains go to from your railway station?
- What type of trains are they?
- Have you been on an underground train?
- Which type of vehicles are outside the station on page 21?

The first railways were built in **Victorian** times. The Victorians were proud of their railways and built grand stations, like this one in Bristol.

Cycle Parks ↑
↓ Taxis 🚗

WHERE YOU LIVE
Investigate your railway station. Notice the ticket office, signs and timetables, and things to help people waiting on the platforms.

Over the water

A ferry goes to and fro across a river, a lake or a **channel** of sea. People get on and off the ferry at a **port**.

- Which is the nearest port to where you live?
- Look at a road map and find out to which countries ferries go from Britain.
- What people work on boats and ships?

Huge ferries go from Britain's main ports. They carry people and their vehicles to other countries in Europe.

Other ferries are smaller. Ferries are very important to people on the small islands of the British Isles. This ferry takes passengers to and from the mainland and the islands off Scotland's west coast.

Some boats use rivers and **canals** like roads. This **tug boat** is pulling goods along the River Thames.

Canals were built to transport more goods by water. The boats, called **barges**, were pulled along by horses. Today, people travel on canals mostly for fun.

• Do you know what the clock in this picture is called?

• Which types of boat can you think of?

WHERE YOU LIVE
See if you can visit a canal and find out how a lock works.

23

Through the air

People began to
travel by aeroplane
in the middle of the
20th century – about
60 years ago. Today, millions of people
travel around the world in aeroplanes.

Like cars, aeroplanes are good and bad.
They can take you to faraway places
quickly, but their engines pollute the air.

- Which types of vehicle travel through the air?
- Do you hear aeroplane noise where you live?

WHERE YOU LIVE
Do a survey in your class.
How many children have
travelled by air? Which
places did they fly to?

Aeroplanes take off from an airport. They start by going faster and faster along a **runway**. Some airports have several runways. They spread over a large area.

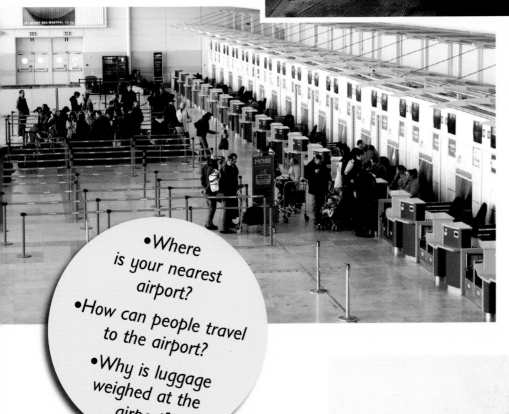

The airport building may also be very big. It has a hall where passengers check in (left), shops, eating places and many waiting areas.

- Where is your nearest airport?
- How can people travel to the airport?
- Why is luggage weighed at the airport?

A helicopter can take off from almost anywhere. It rises straight up. Helicopters are used mainly by people at work, such as a mountain rescue team.

25

Changes for the future

People today travel more and further than in the past.
The methods of transport they use most have also changed.

Proportions of the total kilometres travelled by people in 1955

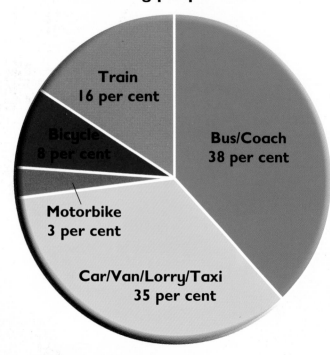

- Train 16 per cent
- Bicycle 8 per cent
- Motorbike 3 per cent
- Bus/Coach 38 per cent
- Car/Van/Lorry/Taxi 35 per cent

In 1955, cars, vans, lorries and taxis were used for 35 per cent of all the kilometres that people travelled. This pie chart (left) shows the other types of vehicles used.

Proportions of the total kilometres travelled by people in 2005

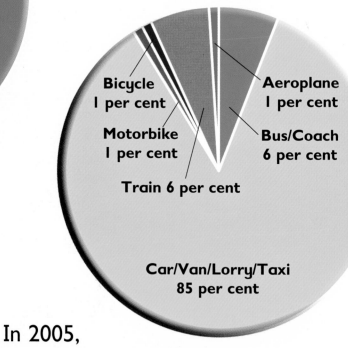

- Bicycle 1 per cent
- Motorbike 1 per cent
- Train 6 per cent
- Aeroplane 1 per cent
- Bus/Coach 6 per cent
- Car/Van/Lorry/Taxi 85 per cent

- Did people use trains more in 1955 or 2005?
- When did people use bicycles more?
- What reasons can you think of for the changes?

In 2005, cars, vans, lorries and taxis were used for 85 per cent of the kilometres that people travelled.

Motor vehicles and aeroplanes pollute the air. People are making changes to stop this problem from increasing. This car is powered by a gas called hydrogen. This causes very little pollution.

You can help too. You may be able to walk or use public transport, instead of going somewhere by car. Ten people on a bus cause less pollution than ten people in ten cars!

WHERE YOU LIVE
Have a class discussion about what people can do to use their cars less.

Glossary

Barges Narrow boats with flat bottoms, built to carry goods on canals and rivers.

Bridleway A path for people riding or leading horses.

Bus pass A card that shows that the person is allowed to travel on the bus without paying for a ticket, or that the person can pay less for a ticket than other passengers.

Bypass A road that is built across land near a village or town, so that traffic will use this new road instead of driving through the village or town.

Canals Waterways that were built for transporting heavy goods.

Channel A stretch of water between two pieces of land. Examples are the English Channel and St Georges Channel.

Diesel A type of fuel that is often used in lorries and buses, as well as in some cars.

Goods Things that are bought and sold.

Kerb The edge of a pavement, by the road. It is often made by stones placed lengthways along the side of the pavement by the road.

Lane A fairly narrow way. Some roads have several lanes marked on them, with white lines or different colours. Each lane is for a single stream of traffic.

Motorways Roads built for fast-moving traffic. They have several lanes in both directions.

Passengers People who travel along in a vehicle, but are not the driver.

Pedestrian A walker – someone who gets about on foot.

Pelican crossing One type of road crossing. Traffic lights change to red, to tell drivers to stop their vehicles. Pedestrians push a button by the side of the road and watch the signals on the opposite side.

Pollute Put dirt into something.

Port A place where boats or ships can stop, to pick up and let off passengers and goods.

Public For all people.

Public transport Methods of transport, such as buses, trams and trains, that people can get on and get off at different stops.

Runway A long strip of ground that aeroplanes drive along to gather speed before they take off.

Timetable A chart that shows when a bus or other type of transport is meant to arrive at places along its route.

Tram A vehicle for public transport that runs on special rails set into the road. Modern trams are powered by electricity.

Transport Taking people or goods from one place to another.

Tug boat A boat that pulls something along the water.

Vehicles Things such as cars and vans, which carry people from place to place. Most vehicles have wheels.

Victorian To do with Queen Victoria. She was queen of Britain from 1837 to 1901.

Further information

There is lots of advice and information about travelling by road at

http://www.thinkroadsafety.gov.uk/arrivealive/index.htm
  From this site there is also a link to the Hedgehogs site, which has activities for you to try.

Another site with activities, games, stories, puzzles and quizzes about road safety is

http://www.bmweducation.co.uk/sots06/default.asp

You can find out about air pollution and how we can help to prevent the problem at **http://www.clean-air-kids.org.uk/**

http://www.woodlands-junior.kent.sch.uk/customs/topics/index.htm has useful information for projects about Britain. You can look up a topic, such as Transport, in the long A to Z list.

To get about, you need to be able to use maps. **http://mapzone.ordnancesurvey.co.uk/** is a free site that aims to teach you mapping skills in a fun way.

Many local museums have sections about transport in the past. Some special transport museums are:

London's Transport Museum
  http://www.ltmuseum.co.uk/
  You can also visit the virtual museum on the website.

The National Cycle Collection, Powys, Wales
  http://www.cyclemuseum.org.uk/

The National Railway Museum, York
  http://www.nrm.org.uk/home/home.asp

The Grampian Transport Museum, Aberdeenshire
  http://www.gtm.org.uk/
  There is an interesting gallery of pictures on the website.

South Yorkshire Aircraft Museum
  http://www.aeroventure.org.uk/

At the Beamish Open Air Museum, you can travel in trams, carriages and trains from the past. See **http://www.beamish.org.uk/**

In places around Britain, there are some old railway lines where you can travel on an old steam train. For example, the Ffestiniog Railway in Wales:

http://www.ffestiniograilway.co.uk/index.asp

Books

Follow the Map series: Bike Ride, Deborah Chancellor, 2005 (Franklin Watts)

Follow the Map series: Car Journey, Deborah Chancellor, 2005 (Franklin Watts)

Follow the Map series: Going for a Walk, Deborah Chancellor, 2005 (Franklin Watts)

Follow the Map series: Train Journey, Deborah Chancellor, 2005 (Franklin Watts)

I Can Help Clean Our Air, Viv Smith, 2001 (Franklin Watts)

One World: On the Move, Valerie Guin, 2007 (Franklin Watts)

Safety First: On the Road, Ruth Thomson, 2004 (Franklin Watts)

Safety First: On Your Bike, Ruth Thomson, 2004 (Franklin Watts)

Start-Up Geography: Journey to School, Anna Lee, 2004 (Evans Publishing)

When I'm at Work: Bus Driver, Sue Barraclough, 2002 (Franklin Watts)

Index